ROUND TRIP

A Short-Term Missions Documentary and Curriculum

www.ChristianVisionProject.com

www.RoundTripMissions.com

Credits
Author: Chris Blumhofer
Creative Development Editor: Roxanne Wieman
Associate Editor: Rachel Willoughby
Consulting Editors: Andy Crouch and Dave Livermore
Executive Editor: Amy Simpson
Cover and Interior Design: Mary Bellus

10 9 8 7 6 5 4 3 2 1   17 16 15 14 13 12 11 10 09 08

Printed in the United States of America.

Table of Contents

INTRODUCTION

How to use *Round Trip* to prepare for short-term missions.

Welcome to *Round Trip*! This resource comes to you from many people who are passionate about short-term missions. As you and your team prepare to serve Christ in another part of the world, *Round Trip* joins you in the process, walking through the major stages of preparation and planning. All short-term missions trips require a lot of work. An excellent trip requires something more. *Round Trip* provides the guided reflection and expert advice that make the difference.

The question at the heart of *Round Trip* is this "How can these short trips lead to lasting change?"

As you embark on the months-long journey of answering that question, it's our prayer that God would shape and stretch you in ways you never thought possible—by bringing you into contact with Christian sisters and brothers around the world, by teaching you new lessons, and by helping you *unlearn* old lessons that no longer ring true. This is our hope and prayer for you, in the name of Christ, the Hope of all people.

SHORT-TERM MISSIONS, LASTING CHANGE

This is what is written: The Christ will suffer and rise from the dead on the third day, and repentance and forgiveness of sins will be preached in his name to all nations, beginning at Jerusalem. You are witnesses of these things.
❋ Luke 24:46-48

But you will receive power when the Holy Spirit has come upon you; and will be my witnesses in Jerusalem, in all Judea and Samaria, and to the ends of the earth.
❋ Acts 1:8

➡GOALS
By the end of this session, you will have:

- Been introduced to the trip you're planning to go on and the schedule for getting ready

- Begun working together with and interacting with your team

- Started thinking about the cross-cultural nature of your missions trip

➡PREPARE

- Take a few minutes and read through what will happen in Session 1. You don't have to write down answers for the discussion questions before you meet, but spend at least a few minutes reflecting on these:

  - Why am I interested in going on this missions trip?

  - What am I most excited about?

  - What am I most unsure of?

  - How do I want to be different when I return?

■ This is a great time to start asking your leader questions about the trip. He or she may not have all the answers for you today (in fact, Session 2 is devoted to addressing many of them), but feel free to ask them anyway. There is space provided for these on page 15.

■ Bring your calendar. Your leader will need to plan future team meetings, and this will be a big help.

> "How can these short trips lead to lasting change? How can they be truly *round trip*?"
>
> —Andy Crouch

▶▶GATHER

Welcome to your first meeting. Once everyone has arrived, sit together and make introductions. As you do, answer one of the following questions:

1. What's the most interesting vacation you've taken?

2. What's your idea of great ethnic cuisine?

OPENING ACTIVITY

Split into groups of 4–5 people and discuss these questions:

- What is your background with short-term missions?

- Why are you interested in this trip in particular?

FOCUS & REFLECT

Watch Session 1 of the *Round Trip* DVD in its entirety (about 25 minutes).

As you watch, use the space below to write down anything in the video that sticks out to you—for example, any scenes that you find moving or interesting, any statements or statistics that grab your attention. Use the space below to take notes.

Notes:

____

____

____

____

____

Notes:

____

____

____

____

____

____

____

____

Share your thoughts on these ideas and statements from the DVD.

- What do you think is the benefit of having a partnership between churches like the one shown in the film between Chapel Hill Bible Church and Nairobi Chapel?

- *"We cannot afford as the African church to only receive, receive, receive… for years we have received and felt no obligation to give back."* —Oscar Muriu

  How might this statement impact the way we interact with the people we're going to serve?

- How do you react to this statement: *"It's so easy in this culture [American culture] to forget to do basic things… like reading my Bible and praying"*? —Ken Oloo. Have you experienced this in your own life? How could this tendency impact you both during and after the trip?

- Consider again Rebecca Stevenson's first statement—*"I think we have some trepidation about the slums: what it will mean to be there; what it will mean to see that; what it will mean to come home after that."* Does her apprehension about encountering poverty resonate with you? What other parts of the trip are you nervous about?

- What do you think it will take for a short-term trip to create lasting impact in your life? In the lives of those you visit?

APPLY

In the video, members from both teams shared why they thought it was important to be part of short-term missions. Not only that, they each had goals for what they hoped to get out of their missions trip or to share with the people they were serving.

Split into groups of 2–3 people, and let each person share his or her answers to these questions:

- Did you notice how the teams shared what God was doing in their church at home? What would you say if someone asked you to talk about what God is doing in your hometown?

■ In what ways has God prepared you for this trip?

■ What are you hoping to gain from this trip?

■ What are you hoping that others, both at home and overseas, gain from your involvement in this trip?

When you're done, come back together as a group and share some of the things that you talked about with your partner(s).

ORGANIZE

Now is the time for some Q & A about your trip. Use the space below to write down any questions that you have or information that you need to remember.

> "Cast your cares on the LORD and he will sustain you; he will never let the righteous fall."
>
> —PSALM 55:22

PRAY

As you wrap up, do so in a time of group prayer. Be sure to pray for the people and the place that you're serving, as well as for the other members of your team.

Requests:

my journal

Before you meet again...

Write a letter to yourself—one that explains how God prepared you for this trip, why you feel it's important to go, and how you'd like to come back different.

THE PREPARATIONS

Commit to the Lord whatever you do, and your plans will succeed.
Proverbs 16:3

Therefore, prepare your minds for action; be self-controlled; set your hope fully on the grace to be given you when Jesus Christ is revealed.
1 Peter 1:13

➠GOALS

By the end of this session, you will have:

- A grasp on the practical things you need to address so you can go on your missions trip

- Discussed the values that will characterize your team's preparation

- Begun the most important work of preparation for missions: getting your heart ready for service

➠PREPARE

- This is *the meeting* for your team to talk about the practical aspects of your missions trip. Plan to ask questions and take notes.

➠GATHER

Crossing cultures can be challenging and confusing. It can also be the source for a really good story. Start this session by splitting into groups of 3-4. In your small groups, share about a time you were caught in a cross-cultural exchange that ended in a good laugh.

As this session continues, we're going to answer two big questions:

1. What do I need to do before we leave?

2. What does it mean for me to go on this trip—what are the responsibilities that accompany cross-cultural missions?

FOCUS & REFLECT

Chapter 1. Watch chapter 1 of Session 2, "The Details," (about 5 minutes). As you watch, write down answers to the following questions. Your team will discuss these answers before going on to chapter 2.

- What differences in preparation did you notice between the American team and the Kenyan team?

- What kind of responsibility comes with being able to travel more easily than many other people in the world?

- What are some ways our group can balance a concern for health and hygiene with sensitivities to the people we're visiting? Give an example of what this may look like.

As your leader presents the logistical aspects of your trip, feel free to take notes, write reminders, and jot down questions in the space provided below.

- Travel information (passports, visas):

- Health information (immunizations):

- Financial support:

- Spiritual support:

"The Apostle Paul referred to his supporters as "partners in the gospel" (Phil. 1:6). That's what you're seeking as you recruit supporters: friends who will pray for God to work in your heart and in the culture where you're serving. This trip will form you spiritually. Invest in that formation by enlisting spiritual supporters."

Note: *Your Participant's Guide is equipped to help you plan all of these logistics. Refer to the Appendix to find the "Planning Supporters" worksheet, which will help you identify the people who you can ask for prayer and financial support. While you're back there, look at the Planning Calendar and the Sample Support Letter.*

Take 10–15 minutes and write down the names of friends, family, and co-workers who you can invite to support you on this missions trip.

When you come back together, think through these questions with your group:

- What are some fundraisers that we could put on at our church or in our community to build support?

- How much can you contribute to support yourself on this trip?

Before you move on, share your answers to the questions from the video.

Chapter 2. Watch the next chapter, "The Things You Bring," (about 5 minutes) and review the packing list that your leader passes out.

Take a moment to speak about the importance of what you pack— not just for the sake of comfort and convenience while travelling, but also because of the symbolic value of our clothes and possessions. Go through this activity with your team:

Look at the 5 items that your leader sets out in front of your group, and talk about each of them in light of Tim Dearborn's observation— "There's a lifestyle component to [the things we pack]."

For each item, talk about (1) what this item communicates in our culture, and (2) what it might communicate in the culture we're visiting.

Discuss as a team what your philosophy of packing will be. As a group, come to an agreement on how to complete this statement:

"We've found that Americans want their space. They want to be picked from a hotel in the morning and be dropped back in the evening. And they can afford to pay for their space... They can, in a sense, travel with a little bubble of America around them."

—Oscar Muriu

- The things we pack will…

Two of the experts in the video caution against giving gifts, which can inadvertently disrupt a community or reinforce a culture of begging and dependence.

There were two main examples of gift-giving in the video. Both women gave gifts to the girls they sponsor: Vickie gave her sponsored child some stuffed animals and a bracelet. Jenny gave her sponsored child a photograph of herself.

■ What are the differences between these two gifts—the toys and the photograph? What significance can you attach to the differences?

Before you move on, take a moment to develop a philosophy of gift-giving for your team. As a group, come to an agreement on how to complete this statement:

■ Any gifts we bring will…

Chapter 3. Watch the final chapter in this session, "Prepare Your Heart and Mind," (about 5 minutes). As you watch, take notes on what kind of attitude to pursue and prayers to offer up. Pay special attention to the key ideas that are brought up.

- What are the key ideas?

- What kinds of prayers are recommended?

- What do the speakers say about relationships?

When the clip is over, talk about the key words and recommendations that stood out to you in the video.

After everyone has shared, discuss these practical questions:

- What can we do to prepare our attitudes?

- What can we do to prepare our minds?

- What can we be praying for as we prepare?

Before you wrap up, develop one more philosophy: a philosophy of preparation. As a group, come to an agreement on how to complete this statement:

- Our individual and team preparation will be characterized by…

APPLY

Your team has just soaked in a lot of information and discussed issues that will have a big impact on your missions trip. Before you dive into any logistics you did not cover earlier, finish up this part of your meeting with prayer.

Requests:

ORGANIZE

Use the space below to write down any tasks your leader gives you before your next meeting.

Before you meet again...

Set aside 30 minutes of time to pray in which you can sit quietly before God and lift up the needs you face, the needs of your team, and the needs of the people you're visiting.

CROSS-CULTURAL ENCOUNTERS

You are worthy to take the scroll and to open its seals, because you were slain, and with your blood you purchased men for God from every tribe and language and people and nation. You have made them to be a kingdom of priests to serve our God, and they will reign on the earth.
Revelation 5:9–10

▶▶GOALS

By the end of this session, you will have:

- Reflected on the unique model that we, as Christians, possess for crossing cultures

- Considered the strengths and weaknesses of your own culture, as well as the culture you're visiting

- Committed to a few concrete strategies for relating to the people you will be serving

▶▶PREPARE

- Read Andy Crouch's interview with Bishop David Zac Niringiye, "Experiencing Life at the Margins," located in the back of this book. It provides an important background to the issues covered in this session.

- By this point, you should be well on your way toward raising the spiritual and financial support you need, as well as getting immunizations and your passport, and taking care of other logistics. If you're facing any challenges, or if you have any questions, be sure to bring them up at this meeting.

- Bring your Bible to this meeting.

➡ GATHER

After you've started with prayer, each person in your group will read aloud one of the passages below, and then you'll discuss the question that follows.

- Psalm 47:1–2
- Psalm 86:8–10
- Isaiah 1:2–5
- Isaiah 56:6–8
- Matthew 12:15–21
- Luke 2:8–11
- Acts 1:6–8
- Acts 2:1–12
- Romans 1:5–6
- Romans 15:8–12
- Revelation 1:5b–8
- Revelation 5:9–10

The Bible tells us that all the Gentiles—that is, people from all nations—will come to worship God. How do you expect our missions trip to give us a taste of what God is bringing about through all the nations on earth?

FOCUS & REFLECT

Chapter 1. Watch chapter 1, "Divinely Different," of Session 3 on the *Round Trip* DVD (about 4 minutes), and discuss these questions:

- What things have you heard about the culture you'll be traveling to?

- Reflect on Dave Livermore's statement, "I have things to learn about the character of God by the way that he's mirrored in cultures around the world." What lessons have you learned by observing how other cultures practice their faith in God?

- How is God mirrored in our culture?

- How should the fact that Jesus "[took] the very nature of a servant" (Phil. 2:7) change the way we serve others, especially in cross-cultural settings?

- Sometimes cross-cultural experiences are dramatic— worshiping like you've never done before or wearing clothing that you never imagined you'd put on. Often, however, the most important moments of cross-cultural exchange occur during the regular "stuff" of life, especially eating.

Break up into groups of 3–4 and have everyone share a significant memory of a meal with their smaller group. Discuss the traditions that your families or friends have developed around mealtimes and the importance those traditions have held for you.

■ Why do you think mealtimes are sensitive cross-cultural moments? What's at stake when we sit down to eat with strangers?

Reasssemble as a larger group and, together, come to an agreement on how to complete this statement:

■ *When we sit down to eat a meal with locals, we will…*

> "On this mountain the LORD Almighty will prepare a feast of rich food for all peoples, a banquet of aged wine—the best of meats and the finest of wines."
>
> — Isaiah 25:6

Chapter 2. Watch the next chapter, "Cultural Affirmation," (about 4 minutes) and discuss the questions below.

- What are some of the assumptions people in our culture hold about the place we're travelling?

> "The first rule is: Hold off on your judgment and say, 'It's different, but it's not wrong.'"
> —Lisa Espineli Chinn

- What "cultural baggage" will we be carrying *with us* when we travel abroad? How does that make you feel? How should you act in light of that baggage?

- Give a few examples of what you think it will look like for members of our team, in Lisa Espineli Chinn's words, "To walk with a cultural confidence that communicates to others that I affirm their culture."

- Why is it more important to affirm the host culture, rather than to apologize for our own?

- While we're all part of different cultures on earth, Paul reminds us in Philippians that "our citizenship is in heaven" (Phil. 3:20). How does that reminder change the way we view the culture of our home country? The country we're going to?

> "Africa's crisis is not poverty; it is not AIDS. Africa's crisis is confidence. What decades of colonialism and missionary enterprise eroded among us is confidence. So a "national leader" from the United States comes—he may know nothing about Africa!—and we defer to him. We Africans must constantly repent of that sense of inferiority."
>
> — David Zac Niringiye

Chapter 3. Watch chapter 3, "Crossing Lines," (about 10 minutes) and discuss the questions below.

- Reflect on Dave Livermore's statement, "How we respond to our mistake is more important than the mistake itself." Why is that an important message to keep in mind?

- What principles do you want to shape your response when you cross a cultural line? When one of your teammates crosses a line?

- What do you think you'll be frustrated by in the culture you're visiting? (For example, the Kenyan team was caught off guard by Americans asking "Why?")

- Reflect on this quote from East African theologian Emmanuel Katongole:

The challenge that Christianity faces in our time is the challenge of tribalism… Instead of living out [the] story of [a] journey toward a new creation, we tend to live out the stories of nationality. And then we forget what it means to journey. It's not difficult to see why we settle, because our nations or tribes or races try to convince us that life can't get any better than this. This is not just something that happens in a superpower like America. Even small nations like Rwanda, even small tribes, have an America-sized imagination of themselves!

Why is it important that we free ourselves from a view of Christianity that is only as big as one culture?

- Consider again the three assumptions Lisa Espineli Chinn brings with her into cross-cultural interactions: (1) these people are made in the image of God; (2) we have a lot of things in common; and (3) these are potential teachers for me. With those in mind, work as a group to complete the statement below. (Try to be specific in your answers: What will this look like at church? When you're out shopping?)

We will open ourselves up to the culture we're going to by…

APPLY

When we decide to leave our comfort zones, we put a lot at risk: the ways we think about ourselves and others; the ways that we make decisions; the ways that we order life and understand God. Split up into small groups of 4–5 people. With your group, take a few minutes and write down the things that make each of the following parts of life meaningful to you—church, work (or school), friends, family. (For example, "My friends and I are very close. We go through life together." Or, "I really enjoy my work because I get to solve problems.")

When you finish, come back together and share with your entire team the responses you came up with. After you have a full list of responses, discuss these questions as a team:

- What do you think will happen when we have important experiences outside of the framework that we normally operate in?

- What are the implications for how we support each other?

ORGANIZE

Use the space below to write down any tasks you need to complete before your next meeting.

PRAY

Your trip is right around the corner! Pray for your trip, for any concerns that you face before you go, and that God would prepare you for the cross-cultural experiences you'll have. Pray especially for the people, the place, and the work you'll be doing.

Requests:

my Journal

Before you meet again...

Read "The African Planter" article located in the Appendix.
Reflecting on it, answer this question: How should the lessons
from this article influence my short-term missions preparation?

UPROOTED EMOTIONS, GROUNDED FAITH

Be still, and know that I am God;
I will be exalted among the nations,
I will be exalted in the earth.

The Lord Almighty is with us;
the God of Jacob is our fortress.
Psalm 46:10–11

➠GOALS

By the end of this session, you will have:

- Discussed together how to handle the roller coaster of emotions that accompanies short-term missions

- Talked about the values that you want to characterize the culture of your team

- Planned ways to debrief and process important events

➠PREPARE

- This is the last *Round Trip* session your team will watch before you depart. Write down any remaining questions you have about your trip; there will be a time of Q & A at the end of this session.

- Read Chris Heuertz's article, "A Community of the Broken," located in the back of this book. As you read Heuertz's article, mark a few quotes or ideas that stand out to you.

- Remember to bring with you any information you need to give your leader—for example, photocopies of your passport, emergency contact information, etc.

➠GATHER

Start your meeting with prayer, and then turn to the article "A Community of the Broken" that you read in preparation for this meeting. Reflect on the following excerpt:

To explain the healthy functioning of the church, the apostle Paul twice turned to the metaphor of a human body, equipped with many different parts, that working together could live out the life of its risen Lord, the head of the body, in a broken world.

But the body of Christ, far from being a healthy, functioning body with the capacity to respond to the needs of the world, is more like a child who is missing a limb. We are fragmented, divided, and ineffective at even simple tasks. Yet, like Grace, some of us are young, foolish, or brave enough to try to overcome these limitations.

Divide into a small group of 3–4 people and discuss these questions together:

- Heuertz describes the church as fragmented, divided, and ineffective at meeting the needs of the world. What will it take for our trip to be a step in the right direction—both for us and for the church as a body?

- Why is it important that our short-term missions trip be more than "sanctified tourism"? What will it take to keep ours from becoming a kind of tourism?

- What other ideas or quotes from this article resonate with you?

After 5–10 minutes, come back together with your team and share the responses your group came up with.

FOCUS & REFLECT

Chapter 1. Watch chapter 1, "Radical Missions," of Session 4 (about 5 minutes) and discuss the questions below.

> "We are not going to another culture because we are gifts to them. The only gift we can talk about is Jesus. He is the only gift we have to offer."
>
> —Lisa Espineli Chinn

- In the video, Lisa Espineli Chinn describes a process by which we go from enjoyment to disorientation to appreciation. What do you think it will be like to go through so much change in a short period of time?

- Reflect on the mindset that, in Tim Dearborn's words, makes short-term missions beautiful: "I'm going to be out of control. I'm going to be away from the familiar. I'm going to be radically dependant. I'm going to be with a group of people I don't know very well. I'm going to be experiencing things that I might find intimidating or threatening."

What scares you about those words? What excites you?

- What promises of God do we have that will sustain us through the challenges and spiritual warfare that may come up on our trip?

Tip: As your team members share different Scripture passages, write down the references so that you can return to them later.

■ Many short-term missionaries experience important spiritual growth while they're overseas. How can we make ourselves open to such growth as we prepare to leave?

As we experience God in new ways, how can we make sure that our experiences stay with us, even when we "come down from the mountain"?

Chapter 2. Watch chapter 2, "The Team," (about 5 minutes) and discuss the questions below.

■ What kind of team culture do we want to have?

■ What are some practical ways we can be sensitive to the needs that we, as individuals, face?

■ What do you think would be an ideal balance of time alone, time together, and time with locals?

■ In order for us to have an effective team culture, we'll need to invest in each other and process our important experiences together. That means we need to limit the amount of time we spend calling, emailing, and text-messaging people back home.

What do you think are healthy limitations to put on how much you stay in touch with friends and family at home?

> "A new culture strips away the things we use as crutches to make sense of the world. At times, it can be a very unsettling experience."
>
> —Dave Livermore

Chapter 3. Watch chapter 3, "Emotional Trauma," (about 5 minutes) and discuss the questions below.

■ Reflect on the scene in the video in which Bill Stevenson shares "the unthinkable"— witnessing traumatic sights of poverty and brokenness, and feeling no way to cope without either embracing the trauma or denying its reality.

■ Are you worried about experiencing feelings like that?

■ Why is it important to deal with those emotions as a group? What ground rules should we set up to process these hardships together?

- Journaling is a valuable way to process thoughts and feelings, even, as Dave Livermore says, the ones we don't understand. Describe your experience with journaling. How has it helped you in the past?

APPLY

You've done a lot to prepare for this trip, and now it's here! But for all the things that you can control—like interacting with team members, being open to a new culture, and raising the support you need to travel—the most important aspects of your trip are out of your hands.

Spend the next 15 minutes in prayer for your team, for your overseas hosts, and for the country and culture you're going to. Take a few moments and write down requests below. Start out praying in small groups of 3–4 people, and then come back together for a time of group prayer. As you get started, reflect on Paul's words in Philippians 4:6–7:

Do not be anxious about anything, but in everything, by prayer and petition, with thanksgiving, present your requests to God. And the peace of God, which transcends all understanding, will guard your hearts and your minds in Christ Jesus.

- For myself:

- For my team:

- For our hosts:

- For the country and culture where we're serving:

ORGANIZE

Use the space below to write down any tasks you need to complete before your next meeting.

If you're like most short-term missionaries, your trip won't end when your plane lands in a few weeks. God will have put in your heart some questions that he wants to work in you for a while. It will be helpful to process your trip with someone you trust when you return. Before you leave, talk to a Christian friend and ask him or her to debrief your trip with you when you get back. Meet a week after your return, and then meet every month or so for several months. Here are the questions you should discuss:

- What was the hardest thing?

- What was the most joyful thing?

- When were you afraid?

- What events shaped you?

- What memories stick in your mind?

- Who did you meet that inspired you?

- What are you doing with what you learned?

- What's happening in your relationship with God?

my Journal

Before you meet again...

Write a psalm. Follow the pattern of a short psalm, like Psalm 121, or borrow phrases from some of your favorites and put them together into something new. As you do, let the truth of the words you're using penetrate your heart.

LIVING WITH A BROADER PERSPECTIVE

Now to him who is able to establish you by my gospel and the proclamation of Jesus Christ, according to the revelation of the mystery hidden for long ages past, but now revealed and made known through the prophetic writings by the command of the eternal God, so that all nations might believe and obey him—to the only wise God be glory forever through Jesus Christ! Amen.

Romans 16:25–27

GOALS

By the end of this session, you will have:

- Shared with your group some of the formative experiences you've had on this trip

- Voiced the questions and challenges brought up by your experiences

- Committed to new ways of living at home, in light of the things you've witnessed here

PREPARE

- Bring your journal and a Bible to this meeting.

- Take a few minutes to reflect on the time you've had and to pray for the experiences that have formed you during your trip.

GATHER

Start your meeting with prayer. Then, discuss the following question with your group.

"Our purpose in going is to learn and to bring what we have learned back... Frankly, we will benefit from this trip in more ways than will our gracious and generous hosts."

—Andy Crouch

- What is one thing you've done during this trip that you never imagined you'd do?

FOCUS & REFLECT

Chapter 1. Watch chapter 1, "Upon Your Return," of Session 5 (about 6 minutes) and discuss the questions below.

- How are you different now than you were when you left home?

- Think back to the video where Lisa Espineli Chinn was speaking about re-entry—the anger a person may feel toward the affluence back home, the spiritual superiority that comes from experiencing God in new ways. In what ways do think you'll be a misfit when you return to the culture and the routine of your life at home?

■ How do you want to go about your daily life at home differently in light of your experiences on this trip? How will you shop differently? How will you view your church differently?

"You know you've changed... and you're trying to have the integrity of being true to how you've changed, but also making sense of how to re-engage your culture."
—Lisa Espineli Chinn

■ Why is it important to show grace to the people at home who don't understand all the experiences we've been through? How can you help them understand?

■ Take the next 10–15 minutes to carry out Tim Dearborn's advice to create an individual, two-minute vignette, a verbal snapshot of one formative experience on this trip. Turn to the "Two-Minute Vignette" section of your Participant's Guide on page 84 and follow the guidelines there to write down the memory you most want to pass on.

When your team comes back together, you'll have a chance to share the memory you'd most like to pass on.

Chapter 2. Watch chapter 2, "Tough Questions," of Session 5 (about 6 minutes) and discuss the questions below. Write down your answers for the questions in this chapter, so that you'll be able to look back at them in the coming weeks and months.

■ What are some of the troubling questions that have been raised for you by this trip?

- Who do you have in your life that can walk with you through these questions?

"How do I live here in light of what I encountered there?"

—Tim Dearborn

- What are some of the changes that you want to make to the way that you live?

- What would it mean for you, like Vicki in the video, to think and act with a global perspective (that is, one that takes into account how your lifestyle at home is intertwined with lifestyles around the globe)?

Chapter 3. Watch chapter 3, "Life Back Home," of Session 5 (about 7 minutes) and discuss the questions below.

■ Reflect on this quote from the DVD by Oscar Muriu, senior pastor of Nairobi Chapel:

I think, sadly, too many short-term missions have been defined by just getting there, enjoying the touristy things, seeing a different culture. And in some situations, the desire is to go to the exotic parts of the world where nobody else has been and to be the first ones there, and there's not really the intention to engage in the situation long-term—to see a difference come out of that situation.

■ What responsibility do we share to make these people, this place, and the work God is doing here a part of our lives, even when we go back home?

■ How can the people we've met contribute to our lives and ministries back home?

"[Will] we go the next logical step and welcome Christians from that far-off community into our world, inviting them to send teams of their own to help us serve our neighbors? Or are we too dependent on the satisfaction of having *done something for them over there*? Would it be too much of a blow to our pride to reexamine the assumptions built into these words?"
—Andy Crouch

- Short-term missions motivated members of both the American team and the Kenyan team to become more involved in ministry at home. What are some ministries that exist, or that we could start, in order to continue in the kinds of service that we've done here?

APPLY

Doubtlessly, there are many things to pray for and to be thankful for as you look back at your trip. Divide into small groups of 3–4 people, then share with your small group how you would complete the following statements.

- I'm thankful to God that I experienced…

- I think the people here would value our prayers for…

■ In order to apply the lessons I've learned, I will…

After everyone in your group has shared, come back together with your entire team and share your statements with the rest of the group. After members finish sharing, transition to a time of prayer and lift up the thanksgivings and requests that were mentioned.

Requests:

When you have finished praying, bring your meeting to a close by singing a song together.

ORGANIZE

Before you move on, use this time to ask your leader any questions that you may have.

my journal

Before you meet again...

Read Mark Labberton's article "The Lima Bean Gospel" (located in the Appendix) and answer this question: What would it take for my life to reflect Labberton's understanding of the gospel? What practical things can I do to make it happen?

APPENDIX

▸▸ PLANNING CALENDAR

Use these four calendars and the lists provided to keep track of important dates and information.

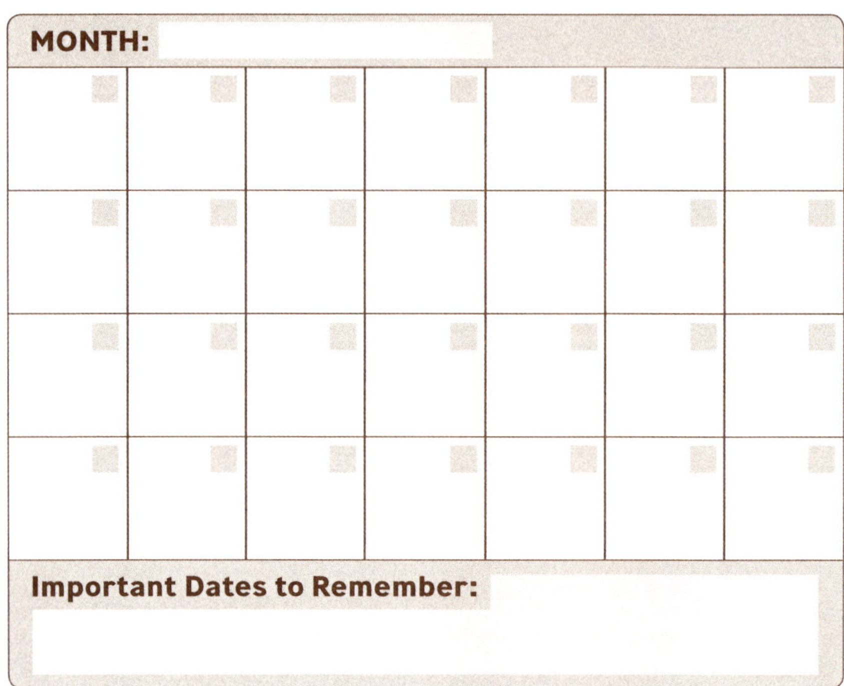

MONTH:

Important Dates to Remember:

MONTH:

Important Dates to Remember:

MONTH:

Important Dates to Remember:

MONTH:

Important Dates to Remember:

▶▶FINDING SUPPORTERS

Supporters are not just the people who pay and pray for your trip. They're your partners. Many of them can't go on missions trips of their own. As you go, serve, and come back changed, they will experience God's work around the world through you.

Below are two lists: The first is a list of people who can support you financially. There is space for 40 different people in this list. These should be friends and family who you feel willing to meet with and write to as you ask them to sacrifice in order to make your trip a reality. The second list has space for 10 names. These people (they can be the same as the people on the first list) should be those you want to ask to make a special commitment to pray for you every day of your trip.

The "Primary Prayer Partner" is the one individual whom you'll meet with before and after your trip to pray about your experience. He or she will be a critical partner in your preparation. As you face experiences that will form and shape your heart and mind, this partner will walk alongside you, approaching the throne of God on your behalf.

List #1—Financial Supporters

1. _____________________   2._____________________

3. _____________________   4._____________________

5. _____________________   6._____________________

7. _____________________   8._____________________

9. _____________________   10._____________________

11. _____________________   12._____________________

13. _____________________   14._____________________

15. _____________________   16._____________________

17. _____________________   18._____________________

19. _____________________   20._____________________

21. _____________________   22._____________________

23. _____________________   24._____________________

25. _____________________   26._____________________

27. _______________________ 28._______________________

29. _______________________ 30._______________________

31. _______________________ 32._______________________

33. _______________________ 34._______________________

35. _______________________ 36._______________________

37. _______________________ 38._______________________

39. _______________________ 40._______________________

List #2—Spiritual Supporters

1. _______________________ 2._______________________
   (Primary Prayer Partner)

3. _______________________ 4._______________________

5. _______________________ 6._______________________

7. _______________________ 8._______________________

9. _______________________ 10._______________________

➡ SAMPLE SUPPORT LETTER

A good support letter is…

- Less than a page

- Personal

- Shares relevant information (especially about your needs)

- Discusses your reasons for going and goals for the trip

- Presents a vision of why this trip is important

- Offers specific steps that the supporter can take

Sample Letter:

Dear Tim,

I'm writing to share with you an exciting opportunity God has opened up to me. This May, I'm travelling to the Philippines to partner with a local church in outreach and ministry in one of Manila's sprawling slums. My team and I will be joining a church that meets in the slums as they begin a new ministry to kids.

I'll be working face-to-face with some of the poorest people in the world. I'll also be doing something I love: demonstrating God's love and acceptance to kids.

During my time in Manila, I'm sure I'll encounter some amazing sights. I'll also encounter incredible hardship and spiritual challenges. I need friends to stand behind me during this trip. Would you consider joining the team of people supporting me?

Here are some specifics areas in which I could use your support:

- I need friends to pray that God will prepare me spiritually for this trip.

- I am trying to raise $2,500 to cover the costs of my travel. My deadline for this fundraising is in about 4 weeks.

- I need partners to join with me in praying for the church in Manila and for the people, especially the children, that we'll be working with.

If you'd like to support me in this important step in my life, please send back the enclosed form and envelope.

Serving Christ,

Pete

P.S. I'll be sending out email updates as I get ready to go, as well as a newsletter with pictures and stories upon my return. If you'd like to receive these email updates, please send me your email address.

⇒ SAMPLE PACKING LIST

- ☐ Passport
- ☐ Travel itinerary
- ☐ Everyday clothing
- ☐ Sunday clothing (shirts and ties for men, dresses/long skirts for women)
- ☐ Light jacket or sweatshirt
- ☐ Toiletries
- ☐ Prescriptions and over-the-counter medications
- ☐ Bible
- ☐ Journal and pen
- ☐ Sneakers
- ☐ Sandals
- ☐ Baseball cap or hat
- ☐ Sunscreen
- ☐ Umbrella or rain coat
- ☐ Watch
- ☐ Water bottle
- ☐ Day pack
- ☐ Camera

*Note: Please do not plan to bring more than one piece of check-in luggage, and plan to have important items like medicine, toiletries, and a change of clothing in your carry-on bag.

➡ WHERE CAN I LEARN ABOUT...?

Passports

- www.travel.state.gov/passport

Visa and travel information

- www.travel.state.gov/travel

- www.embassy.org/

Immunizations

- www.cdc.gov/travel

Statistics on foreign countries

- https://www.cia.gov/library/publications/the-world-factbook/index.html

➡ INTERACTING WITH LOCALS

DO	DON'T
Ask about family.	Ask, "What do you do?"
Talk about your family.	Ask, "What do you think of Americans?"
Share the things God is doing in your life and in your church.	Try to impress people with gadgets or toys.
Learn a few basic words in the language of your hosts.	Assume you know the correct way to address someone. Ask your host.
Greet others the way they greet you.	Take over a project if you think it could be done more efficiently.
Compliment the locals you meet and tell them "Thank you."	Bring up ethnic or tribal identities.
Observe how locals live. For example, if a person has his shoes off inside, offer to take off yours, too.	Try to tell too many jokes; humor is one of the most difficult things to communicate in an unfamiliar culture.
Ask locals to explain what they're doing and why.	Refuse hospitality unless your host explains to you the right way to do it.
Slow down your rate of speech a little, especially when you're with a translator.	
Be careful about spending large amounts of money in front of the locals you're with, it can be very alienating for them.	
Open yourself up to worship like the locals.	

➡ TWO-MINUTE VIGNETTE

This exercise is an opportunity for you to create a "verbal snapshot" of your trip. Use the space provided to capture one memory that shaped your trip and that you would like to pass on to others. If you need help deciding on one, take a look back at your journal for some help.

Experiencing Life at the Margins

An African bishop tells North American Christians the most helpful gospel-thing they can do.

Interview by Andy Crouch with Dr. David Zac Niringiye

As a longtime friend and partner of North American Christians, what have you noticed about us?

One of the gravest threats to the North American church is the deception of power—the deception of being at the center. Those at the center tend to think, "The future belongs to us. We are the shapers of tomorrow. The process of gospel transmission, the process of mission—all of it is on our terms, because we are powerful, because we are established. We have a track record of success, after all."

Yet recently the Lord led me to an amazing passage, the encounter between Jesus and Nathaniel in John 1. Nathaniel has decided Jesus is a non-entity. Jesus comes from Nazareth, after all.

Nathaniel's skepticism comes from being in power, being at the center. Those at the center decide that anyone not with us is—not against us—[but] just irrelevant. "Can anything good come from Nazareth?" It doesn't warrant our time. But the Messiah is from Nazareth.

Surprise, Nathaniel!

What's the problem with being at the center?

God very often is working most powerfully far from the center. Jesus is crucified outside Jerusalem—outside—with the very cynical sign over his head, "The King of the Jews." Surprise—he is the King of the Jews. "We had hoped… "say the disappointed disciples on the road to Emmaus, but he did not fulfill our criteria. In Acts, we read that the cross-cultural missionary thrust did not begin in Jerusalem. It began in Antioch, on the periphery, the margins. But Jerusalem is not ready for Antioch! In fact, even when they go to Antioch, it's just to check on what's happening.

I have come to the conclusion that the powerful, those at the center, must begin to realize that the future shape of things does not belong to them. The future shape of things is on the periphery. The future shape of things is not in Jerusalem, but outside. It is Nazareth. It is Antioch.

If you really want to understand the future of Christianity, go and see what is happening in Asia, Africa, Latin America. It's the periphery—but that's where the action is.

But many American churches are already deeply involved in missions overseas.

Of course. Yet it's so difficult to get American Christians, even those who profess to love missions and their brothers and sisters on the periphery, to actually come and see what is happening where we are. This is especially true of those in the positions of greatest power in the church. I have asked a friend, a pastor of a large church that gives half of its money to missions, to come and spend time on the fringes. But he won't. He wants to spend his study leave in Oxford, in Australia. How can American pastors be leaders if they haven't seen what God is doing elsewhere? Every search process for a senior pastor should ask, "Do you have experience in marginal places, economically deprived places, places with HIV/AIDS? Have you gone to be among them?"

What could equip us to be more countercultural, living in a nation that is very much at the center of power?

We need to begin to read the Bible differently. Americans have been preoccupied with the end of the Gospel of Matthew, the Great Commission: "Go and make." I call them go-and-make missionaries. These are the go-and-fix-it people. The go-and-make people are those who act like it's all in our power, and all we have to do is "finish the task." They love that passage! But when read from the center of power, that passage simply reinforces the illusion that it's about us, that we are in charge.

I would like to suggest a new favorite passage, the Great Invitation. It's what we find if we read from the beginning of the Gospels rather than the end. Jesus says, "Come, follow me. I will make you fishers of men." Not "Go and make," but "I will make you." It's all about Jesus. And do you know the last words of Jesus to Peter, in John 21? "Follow me." The last words of Simon Peter's encounter are the same as the first words.

Can we begin to read those passages that trouble us, that don't reinforce our cultural centeredness? Let's go back to Matthew 25 and read it in the church in America, over and over. Who are Jesus' brothers? The weak, the hungry, the immigrant workers, the economic outcasts. Let's read the passage of this woman who pours ointment over Jesus. Let's ask, who is mostly in the company of Jesus? Not bishops and pastors! The bishops and pastors are the ones who suggest he's a lunatic! Who enjoys his company? The ordinary folk, so ordinary that their characterization is simply this: "sinners." Can we begin to point to those passages?

Yet this ability to read different passages, to read the Bible differently, won't happen until people are displaced from their comfort zones. I thank the Lord for deep friendships he has given to me beyond my comfort zone, beyond my culture, beyond my language. Until that happens, we will all be tribal, all of us.

> "How can American pastors be leaders if they haven't seen what God is doing elsewhere [in the world]?"

Many of us want those relationships beyond our own tribe, but how does that happen?

It is very simple. Come and be with us, with no agenda other than to be with us. One friend of mine by the name of Mark, a pastor of a large church, amazed me when he came to visit. He came for three weeks, and he said, "All I want is to come and be with you." At first, I didn't believe him.

"Zac," he said, "wherever you go, I want to go. I'm not asking what I can do—I just want to come and be with you." So he came. We went to an HIV/AIDS clinic, and they asked us to pray. I had introduced him as Rev. Dr. So-and-So—I couldn't just be praying and have him be standing there. So I said, "Mark, you start there, laying hands on all these AIDS patients, and I'll start here." I didn't ask him for permission—I just told him to do it, because that's what you do. And he did.

We went to northern Uganda, where the civil war is causing such suffering. And Mark didn't ask, "Is it safe for me?" That amazed me. If it was safe for me, then it would be safe for him. He was not unaware of his power, as a mzungu, and that people would think he had a lot of money.

He asked me, "What should I say? What would be appropriate?"

"Just bring greetings," I said.

And I tell you what. He did just that. He was so humble. Of course, there are leaders who come to Africa, who go to Asia, and they come away the same. In fact, they come away worse, with a greater sense of how they are going to change the whole world! But we lose our legitimacy as Christian leaders in an affluent country like [the U.S.] if we can't use that affluence in order to experience the situation of those on the margins. "God so loved the world"—how dare we say we identify with him in that love if we don't go there, if we don't choose the margins?

What part does racism play in all this?

You never discover how racist you are until you have the opportunity to be a racist. The genocide in Rwanda was a very challenging experience for me. I came to Washington in 1995, and some friends were asking, "What do we do in Rwanda?" They were saying, "What do we do with these Hutus, who are such killers?" As if the Hutus were created killers! "Actually," I said, "I am Hutu." I share an ethnic identity with them, as does most of southwest Uganda.

And until I got to Rwanda, I didn't realize how sympathetic I had been to the Hutu cause. Then it hit me. And I began the journey of being freed from that—freed from that history of sympathy for a cause that was just Hutu. Until the opportunity is given to you to face your own racism, you'll function under its power, under its spell. The only way to lose it is to go.

What do Americans need to understand about the main challenge facing Africa?

Africa's crisis is not poverty; it is not AIDS. Africa's crisis is confidence. What decades of colonialism and missionary enterprise eroded among us is confidence. So a "national leader" from the United States comes—he may have a good-sized congregation, but he knows nothing about Africa!—and we defer to him. We don't even tell him everything we are thinking, out of respect. We Africans must constantly repent of that sense of inferiority.

With its tremendous growth, how is African Christianity countercultural?

With all the growth of the African church, we are still facing the prospect of being a religious minority. It may be that in fifty years' time, Africa will be predominantly Muslim. One hundred years ago, Europe and America decided to take over Africa. They marshaled economic power, manpower; they transported their culture, education, and religion. Now sub-Saharan Africa is culturally Western. And Muslims today are applying the same energies to sub-Saharan Africa.

In Uganda, they are succeeding. Muslims are buying property in Uganda; they are sending their brightest young people to law school. They have established amazing charitable organizations. The mosque in Kampala will be opened soon by Libya's President Qaddafi. It occupies the most central place in the city.

The temptation will be to try to apply power, to try to overcome the incursion of Islam. But that's not the way of the Cross. That's not the way it happens. Remember when Jesus and his disciples were passing through the village in Samaria? For many Christians, the Muslims are like Samaritans—a minority that has left our faith and holds to a different faith. When the Samaritans were not hospitable to Jesus, the disciples said, "Just call fire down and blow these guys up!" Yet it's the Samaritans who listen to the woman who met Jesus at the well. Later in Acts, the same apostles go to the Samaritans.

The situation in America and Africa is not so different. Recently, an American evangelical leader said to me, "In a few years' time, it's going to be very difficult for anyone who wants to be a disciple of Jesus in America." But I said to him, actually, no, it is very difficult now. If you are truly a disciple of Jesus, it is very difficult. The same is true in Africa. When I speak in some countries where Islam is powerful, they shout me down. The Bible says, "When somebody strikes you on the right cheek, turn the other cheek"—but they ask me, "What happens when there are no more cheeks to turn?"

Whether in Africa or America, the Cross is not an easy place to be—it is the symbol of our faith, but we do not love the Cross. "Come down from the Cross" is the cry not just of the Jewish leaders; it's the cry even of us Christians. We want Christ to come down from the Cross. We don't like the Cross.

A Community of the Broken

A young organization models what it might mean to be the church in a suffering world.

Christopher L. Heuertz

Several years ago, I made my first trip to Freetown, Sierra Leone, just as that country's civil war was winding down. One of my first stops was a camp for the war wounded.

During the war, nearly 250,000 people had their arms or legs amputated by rebels, militia groups, or government soldiers. The mutilations killed the great majority of victims. But a few survived: Those who had the presence of mind to run to safety with their bleeding stumps lifted above their heads to avoid fatal blood loss.

Late in the day, I found myself on the front step of a young woman's slum-like camp home. She looked able-bodied and healthy. Yet her story was as terrible as each of the others'—her village had been attacked, her home burned to the ground, and her husband killed before her eyes. Finally, she had been brutally raped.

As she was speaking, I looked over my shoulder to see her 3-year-old daughter, Grace, picking up a handful of peanuts with one hand. As a 2-month-old baby, Grace had lost her left arm just above the elbow to the same men who had already taken everything from her young mother.

Grace was biting on the shell of a peanut, pressing it against what was left of her arm, to no avail. As a full-grown man with all my limbs, I still have trouble opening a peanut. Grace was trying to do the same without an arm.

Though my travels have taken me to many unforgettable places, that moment with Grace and her mother is seared into my memory—not just for what it taught me about human suffering and perseverance, but also for what it taught me about the plight of the church.

Our Broken Body

An essential Christian conviction is that the church is the community that anticipates and seeks to express the kingdom of God. To explain the healthy functioning of the church, the apostle Paul twice turned to the metaphor of a human body, equipped with many different parts, that working together could live out the life of its risen Lord, the head of the body, in a broken world.

But the body of Christ, far from being a healthy, functioning body with the capacity to respond to the needs of the world, is more like a child who is missing a limb. We are fragmented, divided, and ineffective at even simple tasks. Yet, like Grace, some of us are young, foolish, or brave enough to try to overcome these limitations.

That has been the goal of Word Made Flesh (WMF). Our community can be found in the sewers of Eastern Europe meeting with children living on the streets, with former child soldiers in the refugee camps of West Africa, among victims of sex trafficking and children with AIDS throughout Asia, and in the shanty-towns and favelas of South America.

It's often observed that there is among my generation a crisis in the theology and practice of mission. For many Christians today, mission can seem to be little more than sanctified tourism. Raised as opportunistic individuals, we bounce from one short-term experience to the next. We keep our options open and avoid committing to any one organization or set of relationships—so much so that many of us would rather work 20 hours a week pouring coffee than give our lives to helping secure safe drinking water for others.

The challenge for WMF is working with those who are intelligent yet doctrinally confused, lonely yet community-resistant, cause-driven yet commitment-averse, idealistic yet cynical, magnanimous yet suspicious, and, not least, over-educated yet deep in debt—and challenging them to establish community with and among the oppressed of the world.

The Voices of Friends

Western Christians are often isolated from people who are poor. This is all the more troubling given the centrality of the poor in the Bible. God seeks provision for the poor (Lev. 23:22; Deut. 15:4, 7-11; Ps. 41:1; Prov. 28:27), identifies with the poor (Ps. 68:5-6; Prov. 14:31; 17:5; 19:17; Isa. 3:14-15; 1 Cor. 1:27-29; 2 Cor. 8:9; James 2:5), validates the authenticity of our Christian life through our relationships with the poor (Prov. 21:13; 22:9; 28:5; 29:7; Isa. 58:6-11; 1 John 3:16-18), and uses the poor as the standard for judgment of individuals and nations (Ps. 109:6-16; 140:12; Jer. 22:16; Amos 5:11-12; Matt. 25:31-46).

As our Africa-Europe regional coordinator David Chronic wrote several years ago, "The poor do not need to be integrated into our community. God is calling us, rather, to identify with theirs." At WMF, ministry is not so much to "the poor" as "with friends." It is a simple verbal change that attempts to honor and humanize those we minister to.

In the same way, in the ministry's quarterly journal, *The Cry*, you are likely to find a story by a child who works as a prostitute next to an article by a prominent theologian; a prophetic piece submitted by a child who grew up on the streets in Lima next to a reflection from one of our full-time staff.

Many in WMF have found that giving up the freedom that comes with the developed world in order to offer the freedom that comes with knowing Christ is hardly a sacrifice.

Many say that the embrace of a child who has grown up on the streets frees their hearts from a bondage they didn't know they had. They see those who prostitute themselves discovering in the pages of Scripture surprising restoration. They see former child soldiers teaching and embodying forgiveness, a sign that the kingdom has come in a small way.

> "It's often observed that there is among my generation a crisis in the theology and practice of mission. For many Christians today, mission can seem to be little more than sanctified tourism."

WMF has highly educated and well-qualified women and men on its boards of directors and leading its communities around the world—still, one of its international boards is chaired by a refugee with a fourth-grade education.

A Global Mosaic

Much of my early exposure to mission came in compounds spread across Asia and Africa. These missional communities lived together, often in a walled campus, creating a transplanted microcosm of their culture and society. Rarely in these communal compounds would I see an African or Asian coworker who wasn't a gardener or a cook. Although these communities were full of dedicated men and women, I began to fear that this model of mission was a kind of apartheid that hindered the message of the church and undermined genuine community.

This is especially a challenge for a ministry like WMF that draws its members largely from college and university campuses. As Michael Emerson and Christian Smith observe in *Divided by Faith*, the highly educated are less likely to express overt racism or prejudice—yet in North America, it is the university educated who live in the most segregated neighborhoods and whose churches seem least likely to have culturally diverse memberships.

Word Made Flesh strives to cultivate a mosaic of diverse Christian community. The staff at its Omaha office includes middle-class alumni of Christian colleges but also immigrants from Mexico and Vietnam. Nearly all staffers raise "missionary support," but some multinational and multicultural staff come from communities that offer support of other kinds rather than finances. Finding a way to sustain a truly multiethnic U.S. office is an ongoing challenge.

Internationally, WMF tries to foster multiethnic partnerships. The Bolivian staff serving in India and the Romanian staff serving in Peru have made some of the deepest connections among the poor. To be sure, a church like Nepal's has its own urgent needs that can make it hard for a Nepali to serve in a place like Brazil, but the more such exchanges happen, the more we believe we anticipate the time when the Lamb will be praised by people of "every nation, tribe, people, and language."

Women and Men as Partners

Not long ago, I was at a large gathering of young evangelical leaders. The conference boasted delegates from more than 100 nations in an effort to represent the global body of Christ. Just under a quarter of the participants were women.

In one sense, this represented great progress—at similar gatherings 30 years ago, women would have been far less well represented. Yet in another sense, the gathering was far from an accurate picture of who is providing leadership to the global church.

As Philip Jenkins points out, today's "typical" Christian is much more likely to be a young Nigerian or Brazilian woman than a Western white male. Women are the numerical majority of Christians around the world. And it is only when women and men work together that we demonstrate the wholeness of Christ's body, where "there is neither Jew nor Greek, slave nor free, male nor female, for you are all one in Christ Jesus" (Gal. 3:28).

Mother Teresa, perhaps the most influential woman of the 20th century, ignited the imagination of the world and encouraged the church to see Christ even in his most "distressing disguise." Along with lesser-known WMF saints such as Jyothi Bhattarai, Daphne Eck, Phileena Heuertz, and Elizabeth de Sirpa, she was raised up by God as a leader for both men and women to follow into service of Christ among the poor. Needless to say, this is an important value at WMF.

Missing our Brothers and Sisters

For many North American evangelicals, ecumenism has come to imply compromise. But in Word Made Flesh, ecumenical partnership is seen not as moving away from truth for the sake of unity, but as moving toward the center: Christ himself. When Catholic, Orthodox, and Protestant Christians come together in the name of Jesus, the body of Christ regains some of its fullness and integrity.

The Orthodox women and men in the community have brought tremendous gifts in the arts, teaching us how to create authentic and tangible expressions of love for God. Catholic community members have an instinct for communal identity that deepens collective accountability. And the Protestants are naturally able to find simple, culturally accessible forms of song and prayer. WMF has found that each of these three great traditions brings a crucial and gracious correction to the limitations of the others.

But when we come together for the meal that is at the center of the church's life, we encounter the persistent brokenness of Christ's body. Two Catholic priests serve on the U.S. board and have made crucial contributions to our predominantly Protestant organization. But at the Communion table, they are unable to serve the elements or partake of them.

Those experiences compel us to pray for the restoration of the unity of the church, and to love and serve one another until that restoration takes place.

At times like these, I feel especially like Grace, intensely aware of the brokenness of our body and the ways we are handicapped in our witness in the world. Calling the poor our friends, making partners of those from very different cultural backgrounds, advancing the calling of women as well as men—all of these are demanding and humbling commitments that more often reveal our disabilities than our abilities.

So Grace has become, for me, a symbol of hope. After all, she and her mother survived. Paradoxically yet wonderfully, even with their broken hearts and a missing limb, they had something to offer me.

Community with those like Grace is a community of the broken and incomplete—but I believe it is also the beginning of the kingdom arriving in all its wholeness, for Grace and for us.

The African Planter

Nairobi Chapel pastor on mission trips and working well across cultures.

An interview with Oscar Muriu

What happened to change Nairobi Chapel from a dwindling group of discouraged whites to a vibrant, international, church-planting fellowship?

They began to pray that God would show them what to do, and they sought new leadership to help them reach the African students around them. That's how I got to come to the Chapel. I was finishing my studies at Nairobi Evangelical Graduate School of Theology.

Any given Sunday maybe ten, sometimes only four people were there! They probably figured, "He can't do much damage."

Did you have a plan?

I knew nothing about church leadership. My core prayer was, "Lord, give me 30 university students," the number I believed was the critical mass needed to turn the place around. And one of the first students who came along is now an associate pastor with us, and several other students who came are now pastoring congregations we planted.

Last year we divided the main church up into five different congregations. I'm pastoring one of the new church plants that's meeting in a tent on Ngong Road.

Since about 65 percent of Nairobians live in the slums, we made a commitment that for every church we plant to reach out to an educated elite, like us at the Chapel, we would intentionally plant two churches that were unlike us, in the slum areas. So of the churches we have planted, seven or eight are like the Chapel, and the others are in the slums.

Is church leadership different in slum areas than it is in educated areas?

For me, planting churches among the university educated is easy. They are like me. I only need to be myself to be like them. The challenge comes when I cross the social divide of status and wealth. That's been hard.

My hope had been that we could be a multi-economic church, where the poor, the rich, and the middle class were together. But it's not turning out that way. Partly because of the location, partly because we communicate in English, partly because of what the different groups understand. When I deal with university students and the educated elite, I'm using statistical evidence, I'm quoting historic figures and world leaders, I'm citing books and movies.

Well, that doesn't work with the poor. They do not understand statistical references; they do not know who Einstein was; they do not understand a reference to a movie; they've rarely seen a movie. So the language of the educated elite excludes them. What they understand, what persuades them, are real-life stories and parables like Jesus told.

We have tried to develop a multi-economic church, but I've not been able to do that.

So how does the Chapel plant churches in poor areas?

I think of us as a Robin Hood, whose task is to take from the wealthy and give to the poor. So we find leaders who can speak the language of the poor, and we link the poorer churches with a richer, more educated church.

I have the responsibility to resource and enable the churches in the slums, and to develop ministries that will be a blessing to them, and to help my members have real presence in the slums as a result of our generosity. We recognize that we need one another and we are going to work together. It's not in the same gathering, but there is a relationship there.

That's not an ideal answer, but it is the real answer.

What's your role as leader in bridging the economic gap?

King David said he would be happy to be a gatekeeper in the temple of the Lord. I consider my role as gatekeeping. If you go to the Ritz-Carlton, there is a doorman there. He never actually stays in any of the rooms upstairs. But he directs everybody to those rooms and assists them if they need help. I see my ministry largely that way.

I am a doorkeeper at the Nairobi Chapel. My ministry is to open doors, particularly for the younger generation, to get where God wants them to be. There are a lot of young people who want to serve the Lord, but they're stuck. They don't have access to the power structures within the church, to resources, to networks, to opportunities, and so my task is to open doors for them.

If I meet anyone who would be a blessing to Jane, who leads our HIV/AIDS ministry, I get them together, open the door for Jane.

How do you keep from being consumed by all your multiplying ministries?

I can only oversee so much. I think it's Peter Drucker who said that the larger an organization becomes, the more it consumes resources internally.

Our church is descended from the Plymouth Brethren, a movement of very small congregations, usually 50 people or less, due to their lack of formalized leadership. They have a council of elders, but not official pastors or hierarchy. That means they can give away a remarkable percentage of what they collect.

The Plymouth Brethren originated among the educated elite in England. They didn't need pastors because they were all educated, all well trained. They didn't need well-developed structures, because many of them were tutored in running organizations. Their numbers were small, but if you look at impact on missions, the Plymouth Brethren were phenomenal.

I've taken this legacy to heart. The more I control centrally, the more resources we will need, but the less opportunity there will be for others to grow and become what they could become. If I'm going to have a lasting impact and legacy, I have got to be one who frees people, blesses them, gives them opportunity, opens up the doors, and releases them to go.

At the same time, in our culture people look up to leadership. So increasingly I have taken the role of father figure to many of these ministries.

Our government is introducing tax-free giving next year, so we're saying to many social service ministries our people have begun: "Use us. If you're independent, you may not have tax-free status. But under our umbrella, you will."

While I do not desire to control them, they want to be associated with me and with the Chapel.

What's your overall vision for the Chapel?

First, we want to bring a million people to Christ by the year 2020. This won't happen just by casual evangelism, member to member. That's important, but we need to do a lot more. That's why we're talking about radio, about education as a means of evangelism, about ministry to children.

Kenya's average lifespan has dropped from 47 to 40 as a result of HIV/AIDS. I'm over 40; I'm living on borrowed time, so to speak. And 50 percent of the continent of Africa, of our 850 million people, is under the age of 15. Without a strong children's ministry and youth ministry, there's no future.

In many churches the bulk of resources go toward adult ministries. How can we construct a church that turns this upside down? In these ways we want to lead a million people to faith.

How do you keep count?

One way might be to give a Bible to each convert, then keep track of the Bibles, and see how well we're progressing. The numbers give us a target, but they are not sacrosanct. We're after more than conversions.

What else are you after?

We want to disciple at least 100,000 of those new converts into positions of power and authority. We call them the Daniels and Esthers who will be in the king's court. At the last election, we encouraged our members to seek political positions. Two of our members won seats in Parliament.

In our poorly governed nation, where there is so much massive poverty, we cannot shy away from politics. We have to get into positions of authority and power.

Also, many of our members are in business and industry. We've got to encourage them to rise to the top and to work hard at changing the way business is done, so it is favorable towards the poor also.

Where does the vision to plant churches come in?

We have a commitment to plant 300 churches. We want half of those to be in Nairobi. Then 60 in other parts of Kenya, 30 in East Africa: Congo, Rwanda, Burundi, Tanzania, Uganda, southern Sudan, Ethiopia, and Somalia. Then about 30 elsewhere on the continent of Africa, and 30 off the continent of Africa.

How do you plant churches internationally?

Getting visas is hard for Africans. In fact, I was supposed to come here to Urbana with five university students. But the United States denied them visas. Crossing borders is difficult.

One answer is the refugee highway. We don't cheer displaced people movements, but if you look at the gospel over the centuries, refugees—

persecuted, migrant people—have been some of the greatest vehicles for the spread of the gospel. Jesus himself was a refugee, fleeing to Egypt and later coming back.

Another track is business—exporting the educated. I tell our members, "If you have reached the top of the ladder here, think about relocating overseas. Open up an opportunity for some of the younger people on the continent who are unemployed. You can go as a missionary."

This leads to the fourth point of our vision: to be a catalyst for missions. There was a time when the West would talk about "closed countries" to missions. They were never closed to Africans!

Africans are not looked on as colonialists or imperialists. Usually Africans enter a society at the lowest rank. We are non-threatening. We tend to be looked down upon. Jesus himself entered society at the most vulnerable point, as an infant, threatened, unwanted—a refugee. This tends to be the door that Africans use to enter communities around the world.

Americans don't do missions that way. Americans always enter from the top. Because they're well resourced, they represent a majority culture. If you try to enter quietly into the city of Nairobi, we all know that you're there! But when I go into London, I can enter quietly—except for the police, people don't notice me. I think that actually puts us at an advantage in terms of the communities around the world that we can enter.

What must Americans learn, and unlearn, to be effective agents of God's mission in the world?

When you look at the Scriptures, Paul's model of missions is very different from the model of Western missions in the last 100 years. The West has designed a model of missions that only works for the West.

It depends on a monetary unit that is recognizable internationally. It depends on a strong economy that has a lot of disposable income, so that a lot of missionaries don't even go to the church for support. They go to the general community, to their networks of friends and family. In Kenya, you cannot support yourself that way as a missionary.

Likewise, Americans enter the economically depressed communities of the world with a lot of resources. They come and stay in hotels. Paul's model says, "Stay with whomever opens their door to you."

When I come to America, I depend on the goodwill of Christians in this country to open their doors, because I can't afford to stay in hotels. But when Americans come to Kenya, they prefer to stay in the hotels.

We are a very hospitable people. But we've found that Americans want their space. They want to be picked up from a hotel in the morning and be dropped back in the evening. And they can afford to pay for their space. They can afford to eat what they want. They can, in a sense, travel with a little bubble of America around them.

But the two-thirds world cannot afford this model. In my own country, until recently, when you left the country, you had to pay an airport tax, collected in U.S. dollars. I'm not even out of my country, and they are refusing my money! And if I pull out my money in this hotel here, they wouldn't know what to do with it. But you pull out the greenback anywhere around the world, and they're happy to take it!

So what is the alternative model of missions?

Well, Paul presents a model that depends on hospitality. When Africans come into the U.S., they go where they can find hospitality. The second largest population of Sudanese in the world is in Minneapolis–St. Paul. When a Sudanese comes into American with no money, that's the first place he goes. Sure enough, he will know somebody, and he can depend on that network of hospitality.

So we want to be a catalyst in missions, to wake up the African church and say, "We may not be able to use the model of missions that the West has used, but we have other models." We can design new models that do not depend on money. We have our ways of getting into countries, our ways of surviving in those countries, of enabling one another.

And what's your vision for you personally?

A legacy of leaders. As a young pastor I was struck by the passage that says, "David was faithful to his own generation." But Psalm 71, titled a psalm of David, says, "Even when I am old and gray, O God, do not forsake me, until I declare your power to the next generation." David was not living just for his own generation. He was living for the next generation.

So as a church, we want to impact the next generation, to develop young leaders. That's why we planned for five young leaders to come to Urbana with me—if they had been granted visas! It's important that we continually invest in the next generation.

Your church has a huge vision. How can churches in the West help? We're used to sending short-term mission teams over to paint walls …

Yes, and after you leave, we repaint many of the walls that you painted! (Laughter.)

Okay, seriously, do short-term mission trips help?

They work for the West; they don't work for us very well. We don't call them "short-term missions" any more. We call them "short-term learning opportunities." The problem with calling it a mission is that it implies an agenda. There's something I need to come and do for you, or to you, to better your life. In reality that doesn't happen in two weeks. Life is far too complex for that.

The greatest benefit is that you come and you learn. Unfortunately, not enough short-termers are listening to the two-thirds world, who receive them.

Americans tend to be very poorly informed about the world. America generates enough news on its own that its news organizations don't have space for international news. Yet America exports so many movies and so much news that everybody around the world knows about America, whereas American knows about nobody.

> "When you look at the Scriptures, Paul's model of missions is very different from the model of Western missions in the last 100 years. The West has designed a model of missions that only works for the West."

So what happens when there is an interchange?

As a Kenyan I was quite familiar with American culture long before the first time I came here. The culture shock for me is minimal. But Americans know almost nothing about Kenya. And so the culture shock when they come is very deep. Some of them see destitute poverty for the first time ever.

When you see poverty in America, on your television, it is sanitized. But the first marker of poverty is that it smells. That's how you know real poverty: the smell. I have watched short-term missioners come in, and I've realized, *Oh boy, we need to go and debrief quickly.* Because they're weeping, they're broken, they have an immense sense of guilt. This is more about them than it is about what they came to do.

Are such "learning experiences" the best use of our resources?

The problem for Americans is that if a church isn't doing these things, it isn't cool, and the youth program isn't cool. So there's a lot of pressure for all youth programs to do this. Short-term experiences have their place, but they need to be more carefully constructed. All too often a church says, "We'd like to come for a short-term experience."

Then they say, in so many words, "We're going to do A, B, C, D, and we're in charge."

We want to say, "Guys, you're coming as our guests."

Do you know that when the President of the United States travels, his people take over all the security of the nations he travels to? When he came to East Africa, the airports were completely taken over by Marines. The local policemen were moved out. The attitude was "We don't trust you. Your people could be terrorists. We'll do things our way."

Short-term missions tend to be like that: they come and completely take over the agenda, the programs, the life of the church. But that's not the way you visit a friend.

Besides bringing an agenda, what tends to distinguish the American personality?

Americans have two great things going for them culturally. One is that Americans are problem-solvers. Every time I come to the U.S., I like to spend a couple hours in a Wal-Mart. I find solutions to problems that I never thought of!

The rest of the world, even Europe, isn't so intent on solving inconveniences. We tend to live with our problems. In America you almost never go into a house where the sinks have two taps, a cold water tap and a hot water tap, because that means you have to mix the water in the sink to get it to the right temperature. You have these single faucets that mix the water before it comes out. It makes perfect sense. But that's a problem the rest of the world wouldn't even think to solve.

Americans don't easily live with a problem—they want to solve the problem and move on. The rest of the world is more willing to live with the problems.

The second great thing for Americans is that your educational system teaches people to think and to express themselves. So a child who talks and asserts himself in conversation is actually awarded higher marks than the one who sits quietly.

How are these traits seen, say, in Africa?

Those two things that are such great gifts in the home context become a curse when you go into missions. Americans come to Africa, and they want to solve Africa. But you can't solve Africa. It's much too complex for that. And that really frustrates Americans.

And the assertiveness you are taught in school becomes a curse on the field. I often say to American missionaries, "When the American speaks, the conversation is over." The American is usually the most powerful voice at the table. And when the most powerful voice gives its opinion, the conversation is over.

So what should talkative, problem-solving Americans do?

I tell Americans: "We're going into this meeting. Don't say anything! Sit there and hold your tongue." When you sit around a table, the people speaking always glance at the person they believe is the most powerful figure at the table. They will do that with you when you're the only American. And at some point, they will ask you: "What do you think?"

Don't say anything. If you say anything, reflect back with something like "I have heard such wisdom at this table. I am very impressed." And leave it at that. Affirm them for the contribution they have made. Don't give your own opinion.

Americans find that almost impossible. They do not know how to hold their tongue. They sit there squirming, because they're conditioned to express their opinions. It's a strength at home, but it becomes a curse on the field.

In a sense western missions has been marked by that. But isn't it strange that Jesus not only entered society incarnate at the weakest point, as a defenseless child who needed the care of his host community, but he also told his disciples: "Do not go with money; do not go with a second pair of shoes; go in a stance of vulnerability; be dependent on the communities you visit"? Isn't it interesting that for 30 years he doesn't speak out; doesn't reveal himself; he remains quiet, and only after 30 years of listening and learning the culture does he begin to speak.

So how can Americans communicate well with Africans?

When we communicate in Africa, we are very guarded in what we say. We don't want to offend. Westerners say that Africans never tell you what they really think. They tell you what you want to hear. And yes, that's true! Because from our perspective, every engagement between two people always has the potential of leading to a lifelong relationship, or preventing a lifelong friendship.

Africa is a very relational continent. It's the relationships that make society work.

In the U.S. things work irrespective of relationships; in fact, if you have a relationship, it can sometimes work against you. In Africa it's the opposite. So we are always guarded and gracious in our communication. We want to guard the relationship. When the Bible says, "Speak the truth in love," we err on the side of love. The possibility of a relationship means I cannot tell you the total truth until I am secure in this relationship with you, until I know that the truth will not hurt this relationship.

You do it differently. Speaking the truth has a higher premium in your context, so you are unguarded. You speak the truth, call a spade a spade, at whatever cost. And if the relationship suffers, well, that's too bad, the important thing is that the truth was spoken.

We never do that. I've had to learn to be more assertive in my dealings with Americans just so they would hear me! I have had to learn to speak truth more directly. Americans have to learn to listen to the relational side of things.

Your church has developed some deep partnerships with churches in the United States. What have been the key ingredients of those partnerships?

In each of these churches it's been important to find a bridging relationship—someone who comes in quietly, speaks slowly, is a good listener, and is trying to learn.

Many churches in America have been inspired to think about the needs of the world, but they may not know of anyone who can play that role. How does a church in North America cultivate those kinds of people?

There are several starting points. First, many churches should start with cross-cultural opportunities nearby. The most important is the racial divide. The tensions that govern that divide, things left unsaid, presumptions, stereotyping, are the same as at the international level. But at the international level they're more easily disguised so that you think they don't exist. Whereas here, in the racial divide, you know they exist, they're the elephant in the room, and you know they have to be brought up at some point, otherwise the conversation isn't really going anywhere. So I think that's actually the first cross-cultural training ground.

A second would be internationals who have come to live in America. They are wonderful bridges. They understand Third World perspectives. They can be your "consultants."

The third approach is to send individuals. We have an exchange program with Chapel Hill Bible Church in North Carolina and with Elmbrook Church in Wisconsin, where we exchange our budding leaders to serve on the pastoral staff for one year. After that year in another culture, they come back and become a bridge person. That exchange gives those individuals the gift of seeing that the world doesn't always work from your cultural perspective. If you send us a young leader, we will do all we can to ensure that he doesn't incarnate into the missionary community in Nairobi, but that he incarnates into the African community! A year is a short time, but when those leaders go back, they can think biculturally.

Are there enough such churches in Africa to handle this level of partnership? I'm afraid once we publish this article, you'll be overwhelmed with churches wanting to do this with you.

In the whole continent of Africa there are increasingly more. What you need to become bicultural is a mentor, someone you can sit with on a weekly basis who will help you begin to understand our world from our perspective. It doesn't have to be a church like the Chapel; it could be a church in the slums that partners with a church like ours. In a cosmopolitan place like Nairobi, where so many have traveled overseas, there are countless potential mentors. And in the whole of Africa, there are multitudes of such churches.

The task we at the Chapel have is to say to other churches, "Wake up, there's a golden opportunity here to craft a new model of missions. So come, learn with us." There is enormous potential for us all to learn together.

The Lima Bean Gospel
The Good News is so much bigger than we make it out to be.

Mark Labberton

Why does the gospel look to so many like a bowl of lima beans?

For those who find the grace and truth of Jesus Christ convincing and compelling, such a question may seem absurd, if not blasphemous. But compared to the spiciness of the cultural concoctions that swirl around us in our globalized world, Jesus can seem like bland fare. Many have the impression that the gospel is small, smooth, and tasteless. They have a culturally conditioned disdain for any homogeneous answer to a heterogeneous world. And they have seen too little evidence to the contrary.

How could it be, some believers might balk, that "the hope of the world," the One given "the name above every name," could ever seem bland? Well, because often the church is bland. Pale. Gullible. Pasty. The fruit of this vine appears to be lima beans. If bland is the flavor of the church, then it is presumed to be the flavor of the One the church calls Lord.

This anemic image of Jesus has many adherents, both in and outside the church. Their innocuous Jesus is the result of social, political, economic, and spiritual accommodation. Who needs more from Jesus than some simple stories of a loving example? To go further would be zealous, and to be religiously zealous is definitely not a current cultural ideal. Those in the church who stand out are often seen as intolerant and intolerable. Better the disdainfully bland than the dangerously zealous.

It's a misstep, some would say, to take Jesus—his example and his teaching—too seriously. To do so is to get too close to all those details that hound religious specialists, breed religious acrimony, and cause war. Jesus from 10,000 feet away is close enough. The Google Earth view of Jesus identifies only the most prominent features of his life and teachings, bringing nothing too close and taking nothing too seriously. Such a Jesus may be vaguely interesting, but he is consigned to blandness and faint praise.

Jesus Christ, the Lord of Creation, Redemption, and Fulfillment, calls the church the salt and light of the world. Jesus seems to have had in mind a community engaged in vigorous, self-sacrificing mission that goes to great lengths to enact costly love, that inconveniences itself regularly to seek justice for the oppressed, that creatively serves the forgotten, all to portray that the kingdom of God is at hand.

Depending on where we look in the world, however, that church seems to have gone missing.

Rather than seek the God who spoke from the burning bush, we have decided the real drama is found in debating whether to podcast our services. Rather than encounter the God who sees idolatry as a pervasive, life-threatening temptation, we decorate Pottery Barn lives with our tasteful collections of favored godlings. Rather than follow the God who burns for justice for the needy, we are more likely to ask the Lord to give us our own fair share. A bland God for a bland church, with a mission that is at best innocuous and quaint—in a tumultuous world.

Is it hard to explain why many look at the church and see a small bowl of lima beans? Where is the evidence that the reality is otherwise, that the gospel really matters?

The Homogeneous Gospel

Others take a different point of view, and think the gospel is too small because its claims in a multicultural, multireligious world are just too particular. Christian orthodoxy's affirmation—that through a promise to one people fulfilled through one man, the one true God reconciled the world to himself—seems by definition too small because it is just too homogenizing a solution. Too small to be worthy of the Creator of the universe, and too "one-size-fits-all" to be the Good News for our enormously varied world.

Postmoderns are keenly aware that we live in a vastly heterogeneous world—of cultures within cultures, of languages within languages, of religions within religions. They are likely to find it extremely counterintuitive that a single religion or deity could possibly reflect reality. In this world of variety, uniform solutions in politics, economics, and culture are unappealing, undesirable, and unworkable. How can that be any less so when it comes to matters of religion and spirituality?

From a theological point of view, they might go on, how could such particularity be consistent with the Bible's own depiction of God's expansive character and nature? Would such a god deserve to be called God, if it all boils down to one way or no way? How could a god who reputedly created a world with 300 kinds of hummingbirds be the same God who requires religious conformity?

Isn't this alleged particularity of God scandalously less nuanced than the enormously varied created order he is supposed to have made? Further, if those reputedly bearing the image of this God are called to one religious vision, doesn't that diminish their created diversity, homogenizing what God has made varied? If there are over 500 varieties of bananas, how could God offer the world one bowl of lima beans?

The Evidence of Love

The love of Jesus Christ, through whom God is reconciling the whole world to himself, is no lima bean. And the only adequate answer to these objections will require us to consider again that very thing Jesus says is central to God's kingdom, the most life-enlarging and non-homogenizing reality: love.

"How could a God who created a world with 300 kinds of hummingbirds be the same God who requires religious conformity?"

The primary evidence that the gospel is no lima bean is meant to be the compelling, sacrificial love and justice vividly lived and humbly witnessed to by Christ's body. "By this all men will know that you are my disciples, if you love one another" (John 13:35). Such love is meant, at the very least, to make our lives more truth-bearing, more soul-enlarging, more justice-evidencing. To give ourselves in love is to devote ourselves to "the more important matters of the law: justice, mercy, and faithfulness," rather than fiddling with our "mint and dill and cumin" (Matt. 23:23).

Of course, this does not mean our gospel will be more immediately attractive or more easily accepted. A gospel whose evidence is this kind of love may still be accused of being small, but it will be small like the pearl of great price, not like some cheap imitation of the real gem.

We have to give up the small gospel that simply confirms what C. S. Lewis called "our congenital preference for safe investments and limited liabilities." The freedom of grace grants us many gifts, including that there is "therefore now no condemnation for those who are in Christ Jesus" (Rom. 8:1). This assurance of grace is meant to set us on the road of faithful discipleship, not just to assure us of grace at the finish line. Such freedom enables Christ's disciples to love because we have first been loved (1 John 4:19). The grace that settles our account with God is meant to set us free from self-interest for the sake of loving others with abandon.

The apparent smallness of our gospel is directly related to the smallness of the church's love. When prominent Christian voices call for protests and boycotts over things like our freedom to say "Merry Christmas," the gospel seems very small indeed. If, by contrast, such voices called the church in America to give away its Christmas billions to the poor and needy around the world—as an act of incarnational love—that would leave a very different impression of the faith we profess, and offer a far greater hope for a love-hungry world.

It would be a new day for our testimony to the immensity and scope of the gospel if we lived out persevering, sacrificial love for people near and far, especially for those without power, without money, without education, without food, without sanitation, without safety, without faith. If this counterintuitive, servant love moved us out of our middle-class enclaves, drew the poor to be included in our family values, brought us to worry more about the need for consumption of those who have nothing than the consumptive fantasies of those who have too much, the gospel would be more nearly the life-enlarging gift it is.

The Size of Love

Love is central in responding to the charge of particularity as well. What do we say to those who claim our gospel of one way, one truth, and one life is too small? The biblical argument is that God's very particular actions are precisely what give us the greatest access to the universal scope of God's heart and purposes. When God's work is most intensive, the implications are the most extensive: "God so loved the world that he gave his only begotten Son." God in Jesus Christ does the most particular thing for the most universal end.

We must make the case that the particularity of love is like the proper use of a telescope: through the small end of the telescope (i.e., God was in Christ), we are given a glimpse into the cosmic heart of God (i.e., God is love). Through the particularity of the small lens, we are given a way to see the larger reality. The specificity of the gospel is the way God leads us to see what is universal.

This is obvious in ordinary experience. We come to know the meaning of love by loving and being loved by particular people in particular places and times. We don't come to know love first as a broad category and then as a particular instance. Rather, only if we are loved in particular do we gradually come to love more broadly. The absence of the particular leads most likely to the absence of the general ability.

It is true that being loved in particular does not necessarily lead us to love more widely. Still, the more noteworthy this absence of love in people's lives, the more we suspect a deficit of an experience of being loved. And that is precisely what millions of unchurched people suspect about Christians, and therefore about the gospel we proclaim: without more-evident fruit of self-sacrificing love, not least when we are affirming the God of love, the more our claim of particularity seems corrupt, bankrupt, or worse.

The particularity of our sun is not a problem, because it shines on the just and on the unjust. So does God's particular love in Christ. The church cannot afford to give the impression that the particularity of the gospel only shines on us. If we love as we have been loved, the immensity and scope of God's intimate and cosmic gospel in Jesus Christ will be more evidently the salt and light of the world. We will be far more like Jesus described us—tangy and tangible Good News. And that is no lima bean gospel.

To order more Participant's Guides for team members, or for more information on Round Trip and short-term missions, visit **RoundTripMissions.com**